Becoming HER

By: Daishanique Martin

All biblical quotations in the manuscript are from the King James Version

Cover Designed: Daishanique Martin

Published by G Publishing LLC

ISBN: 979-8-9918386-7-2

Published and Printed in the United States of America

HEAL HER

Oh my, how life happens. Life happens so fast that we often move through it on autopilot, unable to truly face or process our grief. But grief is not just tied to the physical death of a loved one what about the spiritual, emotional, and mental deaths we endure?

The silent burdens we carry like family secrets, molestation, abuse, generational curses, battles we never speak of. The wounds from needing your mother or father but finding them absent. These experiences are the unseen roots of pain that we often bury and ignore.

In this journal, we take a journey to a place most people avoid but need desperately: the past, the root. The goal is to unlearn, unbury, and heal the little girl within you so that the woman you are can finally take her rightful place yes, even now, at your big age.

Have you ever wondered why your life feels like a constant rollercoaster? Why your communication struggles, why you lack emotional intelligence, or why you walk with the heavy weight of offense and rejection? Somewhere, way back when, something broke. You missed the mark. This journal is your invitation to do yourself the greatest favor: to reveal, release, and restore.

Through this process, you'll move through the five stages of grief: denial, anger, bargaining, depression, and acceptance. And yes, it's okay to grieve. Grieving is necessary. But it's equally important that we don't grieve wrong.

Don't worry I've sought the Lord before bringing this journal to life. This journey began with me years ago, and I couldn't extend my hand to help you until I was healed and whole myself.

Cheers to embarking on the beautiful journey of "Becoming Her."

TELL YOUR TRUTH

TABLE OF CONTENTS

The 5 stages of Grief

Denial

Denial:

is the first stage of grief and often serves as a protective mechanism. It is the mind's way of coping with overwhelming emotions by refusing to accept the reality of a loss or painful event.In denial, you might say or think things like:

1. "This really can't be happening right now"
2. "everything is fine"
3. "There Must be some mistake"

It's not about being unwilling to face the truth, it's about needing time for your heart and mind to catch up with the reality of what's happened. Denial acts as a buffer, allowing you to process the situation slowly and in manageable pieces, rather than being consumed by the full weight of the pain all at once.

What does denial look like in your life? Have you ever told yourself, 'This isn't happening' or avoided facing a painful truth? Write about a time when denial showed up for you.

Think about a moment in your life when you avoided facing the truth. What were you trying to protect yourself from? Write about the emotions you were avoiding.

DENYING THE TRUTH

DOESN'T

CHANGE THE FACTS

What has denial cost you in terms of relationships, opportunities, or personal healing? Reflect on how staying in denial may have delayed your progress.

What truth have you been avoiding?
Write it down as a way of beginning to
face it. How can acknowledging this
truth set you free?

Write a letter to yourself,
acknowledging your strength in
confronting denial. Express gratitude
for the lessons you've learned and
the growth you've experienced.

Anger

Anger:

is the second stage of grief and often emerges as a response to the pain and helplessness caused by loss. It can be directed at yourself, others, situations, or even God. This stage reflects the frustration of grappling with a reality that feels unjust, unfair, or unbearable.In anger, you might express or feel things like:

1. "Why did this happen?"
2. "This isn't fair!"
3. "How could they leave me?"
4. "Why didn't I do something differently?"

Anger can sometimes mask deeper emotions, like sadness or fear, but it is a natural and necessary part of the healing process. It allows you to release the intensity of your emotions and begin to make sense of what has happened.

When was the last time you felt truly angry? What triggered it, and how did you react? Write about the experience.

TODAY I ACKNOWLEDGE THE

BRILLIANCE

IN MY ANGER, NOW I AM BIGGER THAN THAT

Think about a time when you felt anger as part of your grief. Who or what was your anger directed toward? Was it justified, or did it stem from deeper pain?

What happens when you hold onto
anger? Reflect on how it has affected
your communication, decisions, or
sense of peace.

Heal the "little girl" in you so that the "Women" in you can show up TODAY

Write about one thing you are ready to release your anger over. How can letting go of this anger create space for healing and peace in your life?

What is your anger telling you about
what you need or value? How can you
use this understanding to make positive
changes in your life?

Write a letter to yourself or
someone who has been a source of
your anger. Whether you send it or
not, use this as a way to release
your feelings and find closure.

Bargaining

Bargaining:

is the third stage of grief and is characterized by attempts to regain control or make sense of a loss by negotiating, either with yourself, others, or a higher power. It often reflects a longing to go back in time or change the outcome of events.In bargaining, you might think or say things like:

1. "If only I had done this, maybe things would be different."

2. "God, if You fix this, I promise to change."
3. "What if I had been there sooner?"

This stage is marked by "what-ifs" and "if-onlys," as your mind seeks to find a way to avoid or undo the pain. While it can feel futile, bargaining is a way to process feelings of guilt, regret, and helplessness as you move toward acceptance.

Have you ever found yourself saying, 'If only…' or 'What if…' about a painful experience? Write about a time when you tried to negotiate or reason your way through grief.

Think about a time when you found yourself making promises or deals in hopes of changing a situation. What were you trying to gain or prevent? What emotions were behind your bargaining?

What outcomes are you still wishing you
could change? How does it feel to accept
that some things that are out of your hands?
Write about the emotions that surface when
you think about letting go of control.

STOP LETTING PEOPLE WHO DON'T MIND SETTING BOUNDARIES WITH YOU, GUILT TRIP YOU INTO THINKING YOUR BOUNDARIES ARE NOT VALID

-Your Sis

What would it look like to forgive
yourself for the things you cannot
change? Write a message of compassion
and understanding to yourself as you
release guilt and regret.

What has your bargaining revealed about what matters most to you? How can you honor those values in a healthy and realistic way moving forward?

Write a prayer, affirmation, or letter of gratitude to yourself or GOD, thanking yourself for the strength to face this stage of grief. Reflect on how this process is helping you move closer to healing.

Depression

Depression:

Depression is the fourth stage of grief and reflects the deep sadness that comes with fully recognizing the reality of a loss. It is a natural response to the emotional weight of grief and often involves feelings of emptiness, hopelessness, and withdrawal.In this stage, you might experience:

1. A sense of overwhelming sadness.
2. Loss of interest in activities you once enjoyed.
3. Fatigue, isolation, or feeling emotionally numb.
4. Thoughts like, "What's the point?"

Unlike clinical depression, this stage is typically situational and tied to the grieving process. It is not something to "fix" but rather a phase to move through as you process your pain. It signifies that you're allowing yourself to feel the depth of the loss, which is a crucial step toward healing.

When you think of depression in your grief
journey, what emotions come to mind?
Write about how you've been feeling
during this time and what has felt the
heaviest.

What parts of your grief have left you
feeling the most empty or exhausted?
Write about how this sadness has shown
up in your life, whether it's in your
thoughts, energy, or relationships.

How has depression affected your daily life?
In what ways has it been difficult to do things
you once enjoyed or connect with others?
Reflect on how depression has shaped your
current experience.

What would it look like to offer yourself compassion in this moment? Write down ways you can show yourself kindness, even when you feel like you've lost your strength.

What is one small step you can take
today to honor your grief and help
move through this sadness? It could be
something as simple as resting, talking
to a friend, or doing something you
enjoy.

Reflect on the progress you've made, even if it feels small. Write a letter to yourself, acknowledging your strength and expressing gratitude for the steps you're taking toward healing.

Acceptance

Acceptance:

Acceptance is the fifth and final stage of grief, marked by a sense of peace and understanding about the loss. It doesn't mean that the pain or sadness is gone, but rather that you've come to terms with the reality of what has happened and are finding ways to move forward.In acceptance, you might think or feel:

1. "This is my new reality, and I can live with it."
2. "It still hurts, but I'm learning to cope."
3. "I can find joy and meaning again."

Acceptance is about integrating the loss into your life without letting it define you. It allows you to rebuild, rediscover purpose, and honor what was lost while embracing the possibilities of the future. It is not the end of the journey but a step toward renewal and healing.

What does acceptance mean to you?
How do you imagine it might feel to
make peace with your grief while still
honoring what you've lost?

Think about the path you've taken to get to this point. How have the earlier stages of grief shaped your understanding of yourself and your loss?

What does your new reality look like? Write about how you've begun to adjust and what steps you've taken to embrace life after your loss.

121

What you call Trauma was
Training for your Triumph

How can you honor what you've lost while still finding joy and purpose in life? Write about the lessons or values you want to carry forward.

What strengths have you discovered in
yourself through this process? Write
about how grief has changed you and
what you've learned about your own
resilience.

What are you hopeful for as you move forward? Write about the possibilities that acceptance has opened up for you.

Write a letter of gratitude to yourself or to GOD for guiding you to this place of acceptance. Reflect on how far you've come and the peace you've found.

Scream

Cry

Breath..

Sealed in Grace: A Closing Chapter!

As you close this chapter of self-reflection and healing, take a moment to honor the journey you've taken through this journal. You've confronted painful truths, processed deep emotions, and taken steps toward becoming the version of yourself that God has always intended. Now, let's reflect and embrace the next phase of your life.

Reflection

1. What was the most significant thing you learned about yourself during this process?

2.   How has your perspective on grief, healing, and personal growth changed?

celebration

1. In what ways have you grown stronger, wiser, or more compassionate toward yourself?
2. How has this journal helped you embrace your healing and your identity?

Intentionality

1. As you move forward, what values, lessons, promises or prayers will you carry with you?

2. What does the next step in your journey look like, and how will you continue to nurture your growth?

Warfare Prayer for Freedom and Victory

Heavenly Father,
I come boldly before Your throne in the name of Jesus, declaring Your power, authority, and sovereignty over every area of my life and my family. You are the God of freedom, the God of restoration, and the God who breaks chains.

Right now, I stand against every generational curse, every inherited stronghold, and every bondage that has tried to grip my life and my bloodline. I cancel every assignment of the enemy in the name of Jesus, and I declare that no weapon formed against me or my family will prosper. I break every chain of sin, addiction, fear, poverty, sickness, and division that has sought to carry through the generations. By the power of the blood of Jesus, I declare that these curses stop with me and will not pass on to the next generation.

Father, I plead the blood of Jesus over my life, my family, and my future. I ask You to uproot every lie, every hidden snare, and every work of darkness operating in my life. I renounce the agreements made knowingly or unknowingly with the enemy, and I choose to align myself with Your truth and Your promises.

Lord, Your Word says that whom the Son sets free is free indeed (John 8:36). I declare freedom over my mind, my body, my spirit, and my lineage. I decree that I am no longer a slave to fear, shame, guilt, or oppression. I claim the victory that Jesus secured on the cross, and I declare that I am walking in the newness of life.

Father, I declare Your Word over my life:
- I am the head and not the tail, above and not beneath (Deuteronomy 28:13)
- I am more than a conqueror through Christ who loves me (Romans 8:37)
- Greater is He who is in me than he who is in the world (1 John 4:4).

I receive Your peace that surpasses all understanding, and I stand firm in the strength of Your might. I declare that every broken place is being restored, every chain is falling, and every plan of the enemy is being overturned.

Lord, I walk in the victory You have already won for me. I thank You for freedom, for healing, and for the generational blessings that are now being released into my life and the lives of those who come after me. I seal this prayer in the mighty name of Jesus, and I declare, It is finished.

Amen.

I want to speak to the little girl inside each of us. You know the one I'm talking about, the little girl who had to grow up faster than she should have, the one who carried burdens too heavy for her small shoulders. Maybe it was a person, an environment, or circumstances outside of your control that stole your childhood. Maybe it was words that silenced you: "What happens in this house, stays in this house."

For some of us, that little girl was exposed to things far too soon. She learned how to survive instead of how to thrive. She learned how to bury her voice instead of how to speak her truth. She learned how to be strong because she had no choice. And somewhere along the way, she disappeared not because she wanted to, but because she had to.

But today, we're here to honor her. To tell her, "I see you. I love you. I'm so sorry for what you had to endure. It wasn't okay then, and it wasn't your fault. And even though you didn't know it at the time, it's okay now."

Ladies, let me remind you of this: God saw her too. He saw her pain, her tears, her silent battles. And just as the Word says, He left the 99 just to come back for you. That's how deeply He loves you. That's how valuable you are to Him.

Today, I want to give you permission, permission to grieve what was taken, permission to unbury the pain you've hidden, and permission to heal. Those generational curses that told you to stay silent? They're broken. What mama or daddy didn't do for you? That burden is no longer yours to carry. What was stolen from you by someone else? God says, "I've got you wrapped in my arms now. I'm restoring what was lost."

But here's the thing about healing: it's not about pretending the pain didn't happen. Healing starts with acknowledgment. It starts with naming the hurt and speaking life over it. So today, I encourage you to speak life to the little girl inside you. Tell her that she doesn't have to stay in the past anymore. Tell her that she's loved, that she's worthy, and that she's free.

This space we've created together is sacred. It's a place where you can release what's been holding you back, restore what was lost, and move forward into what is rightfully yours. God didn't bring you here by accident. He brought you here because He has a plan for you. Plans to heal, to awaken, and to transform.

So as we begin this journey today, I want to remind you of this truth: You are not alone. God has you, and He has placed women around you to support and uplift you. Together, we are moving forward, no longer bound by the past but stepping boldly into the future He's prepared for us.

This is your time. Let's begin.

About the Author

Born and raised in Detroit as the eldest of six, I was blessed with a strong foundation and the wisdom of my village. Yet, like many, I faced crossroads where my choices didn't always reflect the values instilled in me. Life's trials some self-inflicted, others unforeseen shaped my journey, but they did not define my destiny.

Now a wife and mother of 11, with three biological children (one resting in glory, Denver Rose Martin), I have walked through seasons of pain, loss, and redemption. I've endured domestic abuse, battled despair, and navigated the consequences of my own choices. But grace found me. The Holy Spirit led me to write Becoming Her the first of three journals to guide others through healing, transformation, and restoration.

My testimony is not just about survival but about surrender. Through Christ, I learned to rebuke what was meant to destroy me, overturn generational cycles, and walk in victory. Someone once asked how I became such a strong communicator, and my answer was simple: my trauma taught me. But God refined me.

Now, I am called to help others break chains, embrace accountability, and encounter the life changing power of Jesus. My hope is that through these pages, you, too, will step into the woman God has called you to be.